Written by
Erina Lewis

Illustrated by
Laura Jane Smith

My CROWN

To:...

....

....

....

....

From:...

To my sister Kyra,

Always remember that you are special and unique! Love who you are and the beautiful person that you have grown to be.

And to my parents and family, thank you for always believing in me and for teaching me to love who I am and all my differences.

Love from Riri x

My Crown

Written By Erina Lewis

The morning is here,
I open my eyes,
Sun shining through my curtains
And the birds flying high

I throw off my covers
I jump out of bed
Look in the mirror
And I see the catastrophe on my head

The curls that were perfect the night before
Are now crushed, frizzy and messy galore
School starts in half an hour
But I have to fix my hair
If I go in looking like this
Everyone will definitely stare

I pull and I tug
And I battle with my mane
Nearly in a ponytail
It's getting tighter and I'm in pain
I take out the band and I try once more
The struggle is real
And now everyone's waiting to leave at the door

My sister shouts up
"Hurry up we're going to be late,
you always take so long,
we'll be in traffic at this rate!"

Well lucky for her our mum still does her hair,
have to deal with this every morning so you can't blame me, that's unfair.
I rush to the bathroom and throw water on the frizz, quickly run out the door and
I've survived another hair crisis

I get to school
And all that's on my mind
Is how my hair is
and what it looks like from behind

It's like a knot in my stomach
I feel that everyone's looking at me
My hair is crunchy and dry
It should really be soft and bouncy

It's such a weird thing
To worry about my curls
Sometimes I wish
that I could have hair like the other girls
Some have it straight, wavy or braided
Blonde and light brown, highlights and shaded

Other girls have really long hair or they cut it short
My hairs at a weird length and if it grows it's a reward

PE is the last lesson of the day,
We are all outside and it starts to rain.
My hair is wet, it's starting to get frizzy and grow in size
I feel so embarrassed and that I could cry.

"Err! Look at your hair!"

HaHaHa!

"How does it get so BIG

That can't be yours! Is it a wig??

People start to make rude comments and I can feel all their eyes
The giggles are getting louder and the whispers rise

The day comes to an end
And it's time to go home
My mum is waiting for me in the car
But I just want to be alone

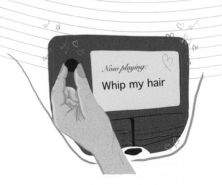

As we drive towards our house
She can tell there's something wrong
She doesn't ask, she just knows and to make it better
she puts on our favourite song

As we get to my safe place
I feel a little bit better
But my curls are still a problem
And I want to sort it out forever

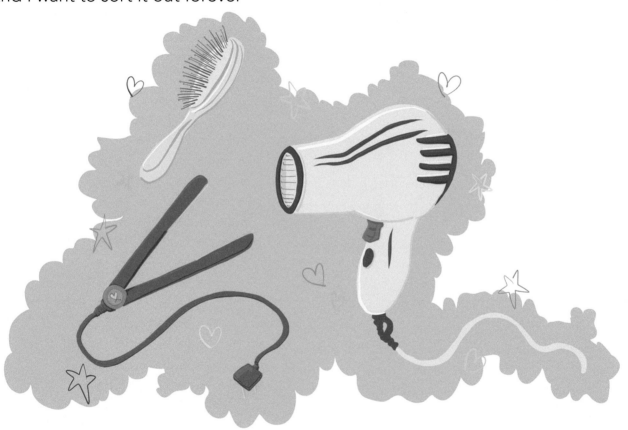

I run to my mum's room and take her straighteners
If I do this then I won't get picked on by the others.
I brush and blow out and straighten in sections,
I won't stop trying until I reach perfection.

It's been 2 hours, one side of my hair is done
But my arms start to ache
Why did I start this mission on my own?
This was a mistake

I try and braid the other side but I don't know how to
My fingers get all tangled, this is so hard to do!

I look in the mirror and tears roll down my face
I wish I fit in, I wish I knew my place
I get so frustrated and I let out a scream:

My mum rushes to my room as she heard my yell
"Why are you screaming? I thought you fell!"

"I hate my hair, everyone laughs at me!
It's too hard to handle, look can't you see!
I'm the odd one out, I'm so different
I know I shouldn't care but no one listens."

My mum replies "Well I'm listening now,
I thought you wanted to do your hair on your own but I will show you how!"
She calms me down and tells me to wait in my room,
She leaves the house and she'll be back soon.

My mum comes back home,
With a bag in her hand
She takes me into the bathroom
And in front of the mirror we stand.

She says:
"At times your hair will get frizzy, but your curls will return.
I've bought a bag full of products and it's time to learn!"

Conditioners, curl creams, sprays and shampoos,
Gel, combs and brushes all for me to use.
My mum shows me natural hair styles that we can do,
So many choices I'll be looking brand new!

I can have my hair down, a quick wash and go

Or a high slicked ponytail so my curls can show.

Two cute bunches with a curly fringe falling down

A centre parting with a low bun and a plait wrapping all the way around.

So many hair styles and all with my natural hair,
I can have them all the time if I have patience and care

I hug my mum tight and say "Thank you for showing me,
I felt trapped by my curls and now I feel free"

My mum replies "You are so beautiful inside and out
and the way you handle things, you make me so proud.
Remember it's amazing to be different that's what makes you, you
And this will give you strength in all that you do!"

Took these words and I remembered them every day,
I enjoy being different in every which way!

Being different is a gift, it's a freedom we keep
Our beauty isn't just on the surface it runs so deep
Love yourself and who you are because that's all we have
And there will be good times and also some bad.
But this is what makes us grow, the lessons we learn
The memories we make and the knowledge we earn.
My curls that made me panic and made me feel so down
Are now my power and will forever be **MY CROWN!**

About the author

Erina has been writing from a young age and enjoys expressing her feelings through the art of words. She struggled whilst growing up with her differences, but never felt like she fitted in because she looked different. She feels it is important to share her stories and show that it is beautiful to be you. This is her first book of many and she wants each book to leave a little page of hope in as many young minds as possible.

AuthorHouse™ UK
1663 Liberty Drive
Bloomington, IN 47403 USA
www.authorhouse.co.uk
UK TFN: 0800 0148641 (Toll Free inside the UK)
UK Local: 02036 956322 (+44 20 3695 6322 from outside the UK)

Because of the dynamic nature of the Internet, any web addresses or links contained in this book may have changed since publication and may no longer be valid. The views expressed in this work are solely those of the author and do not necessarily reflect the views of the publisher, and the publisher hereby disclaims any responsibility for them.

Any people depicted in stock imagery provided by Getty Images are models, and such images are being used for illustrative purposes only. Certain stock imagery © Getty Images.

Illustration Laura Jane Smith
Design by Natalie Gee

This book is printed on acid-free paper.

ISBN: 978-1-6655-9844-6 (sc)
ISBN: 978-1-6655-9843-9 (e)

Print information available on the last page.

Published by AuthorHouse 05/09/2022

authorHOUSE®

You are different and you are beautiful.

Riri finds it hard to look after her hair...
Join her on a journey of learning
how to love herself, love her curls and
understanding that being unique is special!

Riri Riles

Printed in the United States
by Baker & Taylor Publisher Services